Marco Island, Florida.

Published by Thomasson-Grant, Inc.
Designed by Megan Rickards Youngquist
Edited by Rebecca Beall Barns

Printed and bound in Hong Kong by Everbest Printing Co., Ltd.,
for Four Colour Imports, Ltd., Louisville, Kentucky.
96 95 94 93 92 91 90   5 4 3 2 1

Library of Congress Cataloging-in-Publication Data
Barrie, Jack A.
Sovereign wings: the North American bald eagle / photography by Jack A. Barrie,
Lon E. Lauber and others; introduction by James W. Grier.
p.   cm.
ISBN 0-934738-52-1
1. Bald eagle.   I. Lauber, Lon E.   II. Grier, James W.   III. Title.
QL696.F32B37   1990   598'.916—dc20   89-20372 CIP

Thomasson-Grant, Inc.
One Morton Drive, Suite 500
Charlottesville, Virginia 22901
(804) 977-1780

THOMASSON-GRANT

CHARLOTTESVILLE, VIRGINIA

SOVEREIGN WINGS

THE NORTH AMERICAN ☆ BALD EAGLE ☆

PHOTOGRAPHY BY

JACK A. BARRIE
LON E. LAUBER AND OTHERS

INTRODUCTION BY

JAMES W. GRIER

INTRODUCTION

(Left) Adak Island, Alaska.

When the bald eagle was chosen as the official emblem of the United States in 1782, the large, powerful raptor was common throughout North America. Settlers probably saw the birds often, perched in trees or skimming water to seize a fish. But the rapid growth of settlements long ago drove eagles from many of their haunts. Although the bald eagle still winters in every state but Hawaii, most Americans have probably never seen their national symbol in the wild.

I first climbed to an eagle nest as a college student in 1964, after several years of observing them from the ground. At the time, little was known about how the eagle lives; the bird prefers solitude and keeps its distance from human activities. One of a small number of people studying bald eagles, I set out to learn as much as I could, observing the birds from their nests or nearby blinds. For 30 years I have monitored eagle populations in a 40,000-square-mile area of spruce and pine forest in northwestern Ontario, climbing 60 to 70 feet to band nestlings, measure them, and tape-record their calls. I also take blood samples to help determine, through genetic analysis, how birds in different locations are related to each other. Through such long-term studies of populations and their habitats, scientists are able to keep track of the health of this wilderness bird.

The bald eagle ranges only through North America, sharing the continent with just one other eagle species, the golden eagle. Bald eagles nest in large numbers along the Pacific and Atlantic coasts and along the lakes of central Canada and the Upper Midwest. Nesting eagles can also be found near bodies of water throughout the country, from cliffs in Arizona to swamps in Florida and from Yellowstone Park to the Chesapeake Bay.

The birds tend to return to the same nesting site each spring, and often to the same nest. They select mature trees, most often pines within a few hundred yards of

Vancouver Island, British Columbia.

water, whose crowns stand clear of other treetops, giving the birds good flight paths in and out. The tree must be sturdy as well; the nest averages six feet in diameter and about three feet in depth, and weighs hundreds of pounds. As the eagles add new material each year, the nest can grow to be 12 feet deep and weigh more than a ton.

Adults usually build their nests under the crown of the tree, where the top branches can shade their young. The surface is mostly flat, unlike the bowl-shaped nests of many other birds, and the adults pad it with grasses, mosses, or reeds. As large as it is, the nest barely accommodates an adult pair and three young; fully grown, eagles stand two feet tall or higher with a wing span between six and eight feet.

From the beginning of the nesting season until their offspring are a few weeks old, adults spend most of their time on or near the nest, rarely leaving their young unattended. They quietly survey their surroundings with eyesight two-and-a-half times keener than ours, searching for prey to feed their brood. Fish is their most important food. Spotting one, a bald eagle circles, approaches low over the water, and reaches down with powerful feet and talons to grab it from just below the surface. If an eagle hooks a fish too large to lift and gets pulled into the water, it rows to shore with slow, powerful wing strokes. After hauling itself to land, it must dry off before flying again.

The birds also kill muskrats, gulls, rabbits, ducks, and just about any other creatures they can get. Occasionally they scavenge or pirate prey from gulls or ospreys. Depending on the weather, the demands of their nestlings, and their own physical condition, eagles may hunt more than once a day. In winter, adults can survive for several days without food if they have to, and in extreme cases, even weeks. But in the nesting season, they must hunt regularly to provide a steady supply of meat for their young.

Adults tear their prey into pieces and feed their young one bite at a time, beak to beak. As the nestlings get older, the adults let them tear up the catch themselves. Soon they become more aggressive, grabbing food and even attacking their providers as they arrive. The adults gradually spend less time at the nest, perching instead on a distant tree where they can still keep watch. If an eaglet falls from the nest or the structure comes down in a wind storm before the young have fledged, the adults continue to bring them food on the ground.

The best time for me to climb into a nest is when the young are between six and eight weeks old; birds nearer fledging age might panic and jump out. If the adults are not there when I climb the tree, they soon return to circle and call, sometimes diving within 20 feet of me. They usually fly away and return soon after I leave.

I have watched nestlings for hours at a time from nearby blinds. The young birds spend most of their days resting and sleeping; occasionally they preen new feathers, flap their wings, and jump around. They also bite and play with "toys" brought in by adults: pinecones, rocks, and chunks of wood. One observer in Florida has even found manmade objects in nests, including shoes, a newspaper, and a light bulb.

Young eagles grow rapidly, reaching full size and flying age in 10 to 12 weeks. On their first flight, they sometimes stall, crash into trees, or land in the water. In time, though, they learn to maneuver and improve their takeoffs and landings.

Long, broad wings enable eagles to soar on thermals, doughnut-shaped bubbles of warm air that rise from the land. Bald eagles can dive with great speed or skim just above the ground or the surface of the water. They spend much of their time on lookout perches, quietly surveying the landscape for their next meal.

Fledglings remain dependent on adults until they fly away to live on their own. The following spring, some will attempt to return to their nesting area; if the resident adults have not produced young that year, they may tolerate the returning birds. If, however, they have new young, the adults will attack their older offspring, forcing them into less desirable sites.

Many eagles never survive their first year or two. Some never become successful hunters, some cannot endure extended periods of severe weather, and some are killed by humans. If they survive, they will probably go on to live more than 20 to 30 years in the wild; with proper care they can live 50 years or more in captivity.

Bald eagles can tolerate cold as long as they have sufficient food and protected roosting areas. While most

Bald eagles tumble in a talon-grappling display along the coast of British Columbia.

eagles move south in the winter, some remain in their northern nesting regions, living on the remains of wolf kills, other carcasses, or fish they find in open water where fast currents prevent ice from forming.

During winter, birds of all ages sometimes congregate in groups numbering from a few to several hundred individuals; immatures may gather at other times of the year as well. In such congregations, eagles compete fiercely for food, crying out as they fight with harsh calls like the sound of metal grating on metal. In aggressive displays also used for establishing territories during mating season, they soar and dive at each other. One bird rolls over to present its talons, the other closes in, and they tumble together through the air. On the ground, fighting birds rush, bite, and grab each other with their talons. Sometimes the loser dies.

It takes four to five years for a bald eagle to acquire the white head and tail and yellow beak and eyes of adulthood. Nestlings and first-year bald eagles are usually dark shades of brown and black from head to tail, including beaks and eyes. From a distance, they resemble golden eagles, but their heads are slightly larger and they display other subtle differences in body contours and flight. As they mature, individual birds show great variation in their plumage, with patches of light and dark over most of their bodies.

Eagles become sexually mature between the ages of four and six, and they may be several years older before mating the first time. Most are probably monogamous. Since scientists are not yet able to distinguish very well between individuals or between males and females in the wild, we can only speculate. We do know, however, that birds will find another mate when their first one dies, even if there are already young on the nest. Current techniques for identification include banding, color marking, and even tape-recording calls for "voice printing." These and other methods should eventually help answer questions about mortality and mating behavior, but today scientists can only surmise how long bald eagles live in the wild and whether they mate for life.

Bald eagle populations went into serious decline during the 1950s and 1960s, besieged by continuing habitat degradation and loss, illegal and accidental killing, and toxic

chemicals in the food chain, which either poisoned the
eagles outright or, more commonly, impaired their ability
to reproduce. Because bald eagles are predators at the top
of a very long aquatic food chain, toxic chemicals in the
environment can be particularly devastating. A number of
stable toxic chemicals wash out of the air and off the land
into streams and other bodies of water, where they
accumulate in animals at the bottom of the food chain.
These creatures, in turn, pass them on to predators, for
whom the effects are magnified.

Bald eagles are most likely to be poisoned not at
wilderness nesting sites, but at wintering ranges closer to
civilization. Once the eagles are contaminated, they retain
the toxic chemicals. Some birds of prey are not so
vulnerable. Golden eagles, for example, live mostly in
upland areas and prey mainly on rabbits, which eat plants,
so they have a much shorter food chain.

Few, if any, toxins have threatened bald eagles more
than DDT. Widely used in the decades following World War
II, the pesticide caused bald eagles (and many other birds)
to lay eggs with abnormal embryos or thin shells that
broke before hatching. As DDT's tragic side-effects were

*Scanning the sea from a
dead Douglas fir, an eagle
looks for its next meal.*

recognized in the 1960s, its use declined, and a complete ban went into effect in 1972. By the late 1970s, scientists began to note an increase in bald eagle populations.

The bald eagle's future looks brighter today than it has in decades. Public education, increased law enforcement, and a variety of other management efforts, such as changing the way trappers put bait out for other animals, have helped reduce human-related mortality. Bald eagles also seem to have become more tolerant of people, nesting closer to buildings and appearing less disturbed by human presence in general. Now they nest and winter through a wider range, partially offsetting the historical trend of habitat loss.

Once, on the way home from surveying nests in the Canadian wilderness, I saw an adult eagle flying at the same altitude as the small plane I was in. The pilot eased up until we were so close that I could see the shafts of each feather. The majestic bird, head turned toward us, showed no fear of our plane. For a moment, we flew together and the bird's eyes met mine. Then it veered into the distance.

The memory of that encounter has come back many times, reminding me of the freedom and grace of the eagle we should never take for granted. We should continue to learn as much as we can about the bald eagle, not only when it is threatened, but as it becomes more common and begins, with some success, to live closer than ever to us.

(Facing) Sighting its prey, a bald eagle moves in for a strike.

James W. Grier

NORTH DAKOTA STATE UNIVERSITY

*An eagle surveys its cliffside
nesting area on Adak.*

*Rapidly gaining altitude, an eagle
leaves a perch near its nest on
Adak Island, Alaska.*

*Talons extended, an adult descends
to snatch a fish from the ocean.*

An eagle pirates a sea gull's catch.

Head tosses and harsh screeches
ward off other eagles.

16

*Powerful downstrokes bring a
bald eagle closer to its prey.*

(Above) Clues to a recent meal, scales from a Dolly Varden trout cling to an eagle's beak.

(Right) At Potter's Marsh, Alaska, eagles nest in a remote, undisturbed area.

(Left) An eagle and chicks share a nest overlooking Kachemak Bay, Alaska.

(Above) Eagle chicks spend much of their day sleeping, hopping around the nest, and waiting for adults to bring food.

An eagle alights on a perch
180 feet high in a Douglas fir.

*While its mate hunts, an adult
keeps watch over a nestling.*

Near its nest, a young eagle flexes its wings in preparation for its first flight.

A male brings grasses to pad the nest.

On the treeless Aleutian Islands,
eagles hunt from cliffs above the sea.

(Left) Eagles incubate their eggs for 35 days.

(Above) An adult guards nestlings; eagles rarely leave their young unprotected during the first few weeks.

Adults tear their prey into
pieces to feed demanding
chicks one bite at a time,
beak to beak.

At one month, an eaglet is still covered with woolly down.

An eagle lands on its cliffside nest on Adak Island, Alaska.

Still unable to feed themselves at three weeks, eaglets spend much of their day waiting for parents to bring food.

A dark beak, mottled plumage, and brown eyes mark an immature eagle for the first few years.

Although most squabbles between nestlings are not serious, pecking order can decide who survives when food is scarce.

From a perch above the nest, an adult keeps watch over its young.

(Left and above) By their fourth or fifth year, bald eagles have the white head and tail feathers and yellow beak and eyes of adulthood.

An eagle splays its primary feathers for stability and control in flight.

Two eagles search for fish on an
estuary in British Columbia.

A bald eagle lands on a hunting perch at sunrise.

Sockeye salmon are a major
source of food for eagles in the
Pacific Northwest.

An eagle devours a fish caught in a tide pool.

(Above) An eagle's wingspan measures between six and eight feet.

(Right) Eagles gather along Alaska's Chilkat River for the winter salmon run.

Grasping a fish scrap in its talons,

an eagle heads for shore.

*An eagle gains altitude and speed
for a strike.*

Bald eagles choose nesting sites near water and relatively far from human settlement, such as this stretch along the St. Croix River in Wisconsin.

The sockeye salmon migration in the Pacific Northwest helps support the continent's largest population of eagles.

Grabbing a piece of sea lion blubber from the water's surface, an eagle flies away to devour it.

Battling strong winds, an eagle hovers above six-foot waves in pursuit of prey.

An eagle lands to consume a fish
it has snatched from a sea gull.

*(Above and right) Fiercely com-
peting for food, immature eagles
sometimes defy the established
pecking order and attack adults.*

(Above) After missing its prey, an
eagle comes in for another try.

(Left) Eagles nest in cypress trees
along the Wakulla River in Florida.

In a group of scavenging eagles, the dominant one eats first while the others wait nearby.

Hunting with eyesight at least two-and-a-half times keener than ours, eagles notice the slightest movements below.

Sighting its prey, an eagle banks for a turn and dives rapidly to the water.

(Overleaf) Abundant wetlands and slash pines make the Florida Everglades an excellent nesting area.

An eagle grasps a chunk of sea lion.

Nearing its prey, an eagle separates its primary feathers to control its dive.

(Below and right) Spotting a crab in a Pacific tidal pool, an eagle swoops in to pick it up.

A mated pair scans the shoreline.

An eagle surveys the water below.

When food is scarce, eagles take part in fierce aerial battles for scraps of meat.

Chilkat River, Alaska.

A bald eagle preens its tail feathers.

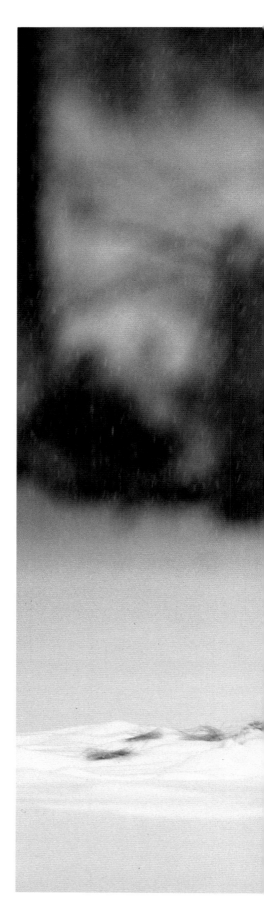

An eagle feeds on a deer carcass.
(Overleaf) Chilkat River, Alaska.

*(Above and right) Eagles congre-
gate along the banks of the Chilkat
River during salmon runs.*

*(Overleaf) An eagle feeds on chum
salmon along the Chilkat River.*

Adak Island, Alaska.

Vancouver Island, British Columbia.

PHOTOGRAPHY
CREDITS